best easy dayhikes
Cape Cod

Cheryl Johnson Huban

FALCON®
HELENA, MONTANA

A FALCON GUIDE®

Falcon® Publishing is continually expanding its list of recreational guidebooks. All books include detailed descriptions, accurate maps, and all information necessary for enjoyable trips. You can order extra copies of this book and get information and prices for other Falcon® books by writing Falcon, P.O. Box 1718, Helena, MT 59624 or calling toll free 1-800-582-2665. Also, please ask for a free copy of our current catalog. Visit our website at www.FalconOutdoors.com or contact us by e-mail at falcon@falconguide.com.

© 1999 Falcon® Publishing, Inc., Helena, Montana.
Printed in Canada.

1 2 3 4 5 6 7 8 9 0 TP 04 03 02 01 00 99

Falcon and FalconGuide are registered trademarks of Falcon® Publishing, Inc.

Cover photo by David G. Curran/New England Stock.

Cataloging-in-Publication Data
Huban, Cheryl Hohnson, 1955-
    Best easy day hikes, Cape Cod / Cheryl Johnson Huban
        p.   cm. -- (A Falcon guide)
    Includes index.
    ISBN 1-56044-855-5 (pbk.)
    1. Hiking--Massachusetts--Cape Cod--Guidebooks. 2. Cape Cod
(Mass.)--Guidebooks. I. Title. II. Series
GV199.42.M42C364   1999
917.44'920443--dc21   99-19752
                                                                          CIP

CAUTION

Outdoor recreational activities are by their very nature potentially hazardous. All participants in such activities must assume responsibility for their own actions and safety. The information contained in this guidebook cannot replace sound judgment and good decision-making skills, which help reduce risk exposure, nor does the scope of this book allow for disclosure of all the potential hazards and risks involved in such activities.

Learn as much as possible about the outdoor recreational activities in which you participate, prepare for the unexpected, and be cautious. The reward will be a safer and more enjoyable experience.

 Text pages printed on recycled paper.

Contents

This book is dedicated to Aaron, Connor, Emily, Dylan, Brandon, Hannah, Casey, Jessica, and Hope in an effort to inspire and nurture their love of the outdoors.

Acknowledgments

Please join me in supporting all of the wonderful organizations, both public and private, that preserve the unique landscape of Cape Cod, Martha's Vineyard, and Nantucket. Their work provides special places not only for plant and wildlife to prosper, but for future generations to discover. A special thank-you to my husband and hiking companion, Marvin, whose help and support made this possible.

Map Legend

Interstate	(00)	Campground	▲
US Highway	(00)	Cabins/Buildings	■
State or Other Principal Road	(00) (000)	Bridge	⌣
National Park Route	(00)	Hill	▰
Interstate Highway	⟹	Elevation	9,782 ft. ✕
Paved Road	⟹	Gate	•——•
Gravel Road	⟹	Marsh	⁕ ⁕ ⁕
Unimproved Road	=======⟹	Overlook/Point of Interest	◘
Trailhead	○	Park Boundary	⌐ ¬
Main Trail	━━━		
Secondary Trail	- - - -	Map Orientation	N ▲
Parking Area	Ⓟ		
River/Creek/Falls	∿	Scale	0 0.5 1 ▬▬▬ Miles
Spring	⚲		
Directional Arrow	⟵		

v

Overview Map of Cape Cod and The Islands

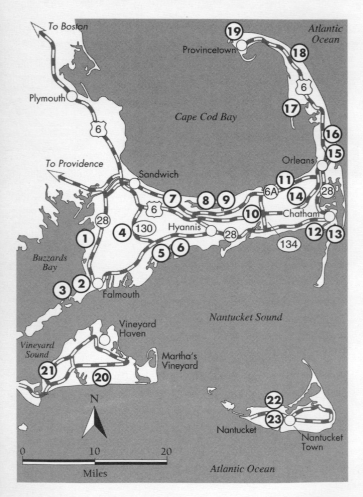

Ranking the Hikes

The following list ranks the hikes in this book from easiest to hardest.

* Handicap/Stroller accessible depending on the weather.
° Marked for the visually impaired.

Introduction

Cape Cod and the islands of Martha's Vineyard and Nantucket have become a summer paradise for millions of visitors each year. Shaped like an upraised arm, the Cape is riddled with ice age ponds and rimmed with wide expanses of white sand beaches. Birds and wildlife find homes in the salt and freshwater marshes that stretch beyond the defined waterways.

Ancient forests, quiet estuaries, and sandy dunes offer an escape from the hustle and bustle of a busy summer vacation or everyday life, as well as a glimpse of the Cape and Islands' varied terrain and historical past. This book is designed for those who wish to take the less-frequented road.

These hikes were selected from the many lovely spots on the Cape for their diversity and seclusion. Though they vary in length, most are one to two miles long, and the longest is 6.2 miles round-trip. All hikes are on easy-to-follow trails and you can reach all trailheads in a regular passenger car.

Some of the hikes in this book will challenge the physically fit, others are easy enough for young children and some are accessible to people with disabilities (depending on the weather.) The Cape and the islands are relatively flat; the majority of hikes have only minor changes in elevation, and the largest climb gains a total of 158 feet.

To help you decide on the right trail, I've ranked the hikes from easiest to hardest. Please keep in mind that long does not always equal difficult. Other factors, such as elevation gain, soft sand, and other trail conditions, have to be considered. To approximate how long it will take you to complete a given trail, use the standard of two miles per hour, adding time if you are not a strong hiker or are traveling with small children, and subtracting time if you are in good shape. Add time for picnics, rest stops, or other activities you plan for your outing.

Detailed maps may be available at some of the trailheads and the pertinent USGS topographical map is listed with each hike. Unfortunately, the USGS maps are dated, and many of the hikes are not shown, but general location and direction are noted.

I hope you thoroughly enjoy your "best easy" hiking journey through the natural wonders of Cape Cod and The Islands.

—*Cheryl Huban*

Leave No Trace

The delicate balance between water and land on Cape Cod and the Islands can accommodate human use as long as everybody treats it with respect. Just as you would never think of leaving your mark on a treasured piece of artwork in a museum, refrain from leaving any trace of yourself on nature's artwork.

The need for good manners applies to all visitors, those from far away as well as those who live next door. A few thoughtless or uninformed hikers can ruin a pristine landscape for everyone who follows. The book *Leave No Trace* is a valuable resource for learning more about the principles of environmentally friendly use of our land resources.

Three FalconGuide Principles of Leave No Trace

• *Leave with everything you brought with you.*
• *Leave no sign of your visit.*
• *Leave the landscape as you found it.*

Most of us know better than to litter—on or off the hiking trail. Even the tiniest scrap of paper left along the trail detracts from the beauty of the Cape. This means that you should pack out everything, even biodegradable items like orange peels, which can take years to decompose. It's also a good idea to pick up any trash that less considerate hikers have left behind.

To avoid damaging the surrounding soil and plants, stay

on the trail. Avoid cutting switchbacks and venturing onto fragile vegetation. Marsh grasses are particularly vulnerable to damage. Select a durable surface like a bare log, a rock or a sandy beach for rest stops.

Don't pick up "souvenirs," such as rocks, feathers, wildflowers, or berries. Not only will you deprive the next visitor the thrill of discovery, but you may disrupt the reproductive cycle of the plants. Never take live shells. Not only are you removing wildlife from its natural habitat, but once the poor creature living inside the shell dies, its stench will force you to throw it away.

Avoid making loud noises that disturb the silence others may be enjoying. Remember, sound travels easily in the outdoors. Be courteous.

When nature calls, use established facilities whenever possible. If these are unavailable, bury human waste six to eight inches deep and pack out used toilet paper. This is a good reason to carry a lightweight trowel. Keep wastes at least 300 feet away from any surface water or wetlands and above the high-tide line.

Finally, and perhaps most importantly, strictly follow the pack-it-in/pack-it-out rule. If you carry something with you, consume it completely or carry it out with you.

Leave No Trace—put your ear to the ground and listen carefully. Thousand of people coming behind you are thanking you for your courtesy and good sense.

Be Prepared

Only three real dangers exist on the Cape and the Islands: sun, poisonous plants, and insects. Be sure to pack a hat, sunglasses, suntan lotion—and then use them. Everyone wants a vacation tan, but if you overdo, it can become a vacation disaster.

Familiarize yourself with the symptoms of heat-related conditions. Sunny, humid days are beautiful, but can cause heat stroke or heat exhaustion. The best way to avoid these afflictions is to wear clothing appropriate to the weather conditions, drink lots of water, and keep a pace that is within your physical limits.

The Cape is home to an abundance of wildlife and plant life. It's a beautiful world, but it also can be unpredictable. Keep your hands to yourself. Don't pick the flowers or finger foliage. Poison ivy comes in many varieties, from shrubs to trailing vines with leaves shiny or dull, green or red leaves.

Be alert for ticks, especially in the spring and early summer. These tiny, flat, round parasites are less than one-quarter-inch long and certain species have been associated with Lyme disease. Pack repellant for pesky mosquitos and greenheads, the biting flies usually found in marshlands.

You'll enjoy hiking much more if you wear good socks and comfortable walking shoes. For a beach hike on soft sand, over-the-ankle boots or shoes add extra support.

Carry a backpack loaded with ample water or sport drink, snacks and/or a lunch, and a picnic ground cover. Add a bathing suit and towel if you are beach- or pond-bound.

The Upper Cape

The "Upper Cape" refers to the region of Cape Cod closest to the mainland. It includes the towns of Bourne, Falmouth, Sandwich, and Mashpee.

One of the first areas to be settled on the Cape, each town has a rich historic heritage. Natural resources were used to support agriculture, saltworks, fishing, whaling, and glassworks. Remnants of this history are evident throughout the area and in the names of roads and villages. The Upper Cape also was blessed with farsighted citizens who donated acres of land to the public, all of which is waiting to be explored.

Gentle hills and fertile river basins support pitch pine forests and lush undergrowth. Interior forests of majestic hardwoods, including eastern red cedar and American holly, remain sole survivors of the original Cape landscape, having been spared from early settlers' needs for building materials. Defined by a manmade canal on the northwest, vast estuaries on the southwest, and sandy beaches on the north and south, the Upper Cape offers solitude for all those who seek it.

1
RED BROOK POND CONSERVATION AREA TRAIL

Type of hike: Loop.
Total distance: 1.2 miles.
Maps: USGS Pocasset.
Jurisdiction: Bourne Conservation Trust.
Starting point: Thaxter Road, Bourne.
Finding the trailhead: To reach the reserve from the Bourne Rotary, go south on Massachusetts 28 for 3.4 miles to Barlows Landing Road. Turn right for 1.8 miles, across County Road, to the stop sign. Turn left (south) onto Shore Road. Go through the underpass, then go 0.2 mile to the small lot on the left at Thaxter Road. A sign on the corner reads Red Brook Pond Conservation Area.

Key points:
0.2   Reach the red-marked trail intersection
0.6   Descend to the first bog
0.8   Head into the woods

The hike: This is a delightful romp through pitch pine woods, along ridges with views of the forest and lush undergrowth—and best of all, a firsthand look at working cranberry bogs. The reserve is the perfect antidote for stress—the restful, cool woodlands soothe the soul.

Red Brook Pond Conservation Area Trail

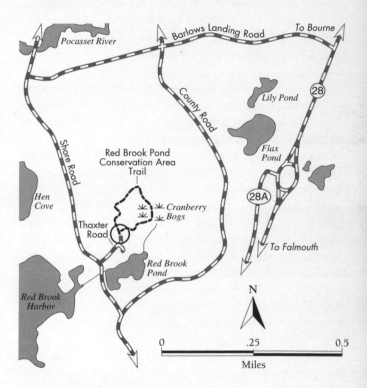

Birds are plentiful; squirrels and rabbits frolic in the underbrush and an occasional deer wanders through the reserve. In the fall, the hardwood forest bursts into vibrant color, especially appealing against the red cranberries. One of the few fruits native to North America, cranberries were growing wild on the Cape when the Pilgrims landed. These wild cranberry bogs were created when kettle ponds gradually filled up with silt and plant debris. The organic layers formed peat, and cranberry vines took root in the top layers of moss.

Native Americans used cranberries to color rugs and blankets, flavor pemmican cakes and succotash, and to treat wounds from poison arrows. Rich in Vitamin C, whalers and pirates used cranberries to prevent scurvy.

To begin the hike, walk east up Thaxter Road, past the basketball hoop, to the road's end. The trail is straight ahead, and is marked with wooden blue whales posted on the trees.

Turn right (east) at the first trail intersection (0.2 mile), walking onto the red-marked trail. Hike along the ridge, passing a huge, glacial boulder on the left. Stay right (east) at the Y intersection and descend to the first bog (0.6 mile). Turn left (north) at the bog and follow its contours. Swing left (west), onto the roadway to the second bog, turning right (north) just before the bog begins. Stay on the road until you reach the trail at 0.8 mile that heads back into the woods, which is directly in front of you.

Climb the hill and turn left (west) at the top. Watch for animal prints on the sandy trail and catch glimpses of the bog below you on the left. The trail narrows through a section of new-growth pines, circling back to the trailhead.

2
THE TRAILS IN BEEBE WOODS

Type of hike: Out-and-back.
Total distance: 3.2 miles.
Maps: USGS Woods Hole.
Jurisdiction: Falmouth Conservation Commission.
Starting point: Cape Cod Conservatory Parking Area, Falmouth.
Finding the trailhead: To reach Beebe Woods from the Bourne Rotary, go south on Massachusetts 28 for 14 miles, through another rotary and past the spot where MA 28 turns into a two-lane road. Continue straight on Main Street when MA 28 veers off to the left into downtown Falmouth. (Follow the Woods Hole signs.) Turn right for 0.1 mile to the large white sign marking Depot Avenue. Continue for 0.5 mile to the end of Depot, driving behind the theater to the Cape Cod Conservatory Parking Area.

Key points:
0.2   Reach the first trail intersection
0.4   Pass the Punch Bowl Trail
0.6   Reach the four corners
1.6   Walk down to Ice House Pond

The hike: This vast expanse of woodlands was donated by Mr. and Mrs. J.K. Lilly III to the town of Falmouth in 1976.

Originally part of the summer estate of James M. Beebe, it is now bordered by residential areas. Carriage paths allow you to walk side by side, and dogs are welcome.

Swampy areas dot the woods and a large pond is a serene destination. Glacial boulders sit as silent sentries, often surrounded by bear, bay, and blueberries.

Many trails bisect the 387 acres of woodland. Some are access for local homeowners, others lead to kettle ponds or pass abandoned farm buildings. Unfortunately, the narrow trails are not well-marked and can be more lengthy than they may appear at first. I recommend that you stay on the carriage paths unless you travel with a local guide.

The trail begins on the right (east side) of the Conservatory building as you face it, and uphill to the left of the Conservation sign. Enter the woods through an area of white pine into a clearing marked with a dramatic glacial boulder. Pass the boulder and turn left (northwest) onto a wide sandy roadway. Stay on the carriage path, taking the right fork at 0.2 mile and passing the trail to the Punch Bowl at 0.4 mile.

Look for bearberry and bayberry, enjoy the cool shade and dank scent of rich soil on the way to the four corners (0.6 mile), where two carriage paths intersect. Turn right (northeast). Stay on the pathway for one mile, ignoring the small trail intersections. At the fork, hook left. The trail narrows and curves around to Ice House Pond. Walk all the way to the metal fence and down to the waterline. Enjoy a rest at this peaceful spot, then return as you came.

Option: At 0.4 mile, turn right (north) and make a visit to the Punch Bowl—a deep kettle pond (0.6-mile round trip).

The Trails in Beebe Woods
The Knob at Quissett Harbor Trail

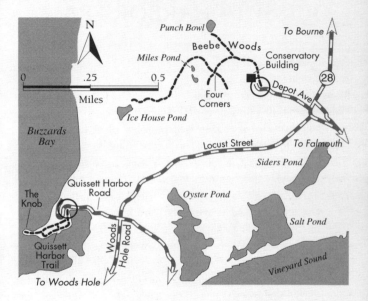

3
THE KNOB AT QUISSETT HARBOR TRAIL

See map on page 13

Type of hike: Loop.
Total distance: 1.2 miles.
Maps: USGS Woods Hole.
Jurisdiction: Salt Pond Areas Bird Sanctuaries, Inc.
Starting point: Quissett Harbor Road, Falmouth.
Finding the trailhead: To reach the start of The Knob trail from the Bourne Rotary, go south on Massachusetts 28 for 14 miles, through another rotary and past the spot where the route turns into a two-lane road. Continue straight on Main Street when MA 28 veers off to the left into downtown Falmouth. (Follow the Woods Hole signs.) At the stop sign (0.2 mile), turn right onto Locust Street. It is not marked. Stay on Locust for 1.7 miles to the stoplight at Quissett Harbor Road. Turn right and follow Quissett Harbor Road around the harbor to the far side. Limited parking is on the right, directly before the road ends on private property.

Key points:
0.1 Reach the bottom of loop
0.4 Stay along the shoreline trail
0.5 Walk back into the woods at the top of loop
0.7 Climb steps to see the view from The Knob

The hike: This trail is fun with a capital "F." It winds through woodlands past views of quaint Quissett Harbor to a child's paradise of ancient oak trees that invite climbing and are equipped with rope swings. Watch clammers patrol a rocky beach in search of dinner. Then, for the ultimate in pleasant hiking, walk up onto a rise above an intimate, rock-lined, crescent-shaped sandy beach and across a narrow causeway of coarse beach grass to "The Knob." This tiny round peninsula juts out into Buzzard's Bay and the view is spectacular.

To the far left, the Elizabeth Islands mound on the horizon. The towns of Wareham, Marion, Mattapoisett, and Fairhaven follow the coast from right to left. Sakonnet is the last town before the coast shifts around into Rhode Island Sound. A marble bench expresses the heartfelt thanks from all that visit to Cornelia L. Carey, who donated these 13 acres of beauty at her death in 1973 to Salt Pond Areas Bird Sanctuaries, Inc.

Begin by crossing the road to the small entrance for the dirt trail, which leads up (south) into the woods. Please stay on the cut trails at all times. Turn left (south) at the Y intersection (0.1 mile) and climb the steps. At the first trail intersection, turn right and follow the joyful sounds of children into a grove of magnificent oaks.

Return to the main trail and turn right (west). Stay left, along the coastline, at all small trail intersections, until you reach a trail that descends to a rocky beach (0.4 mile). Choose the trail on the right (north) and climb the slight rise. Walk back into the woods to a T intersection at 0.5 mile, where you turn left (west). On the right is a crescent-shaped beach, and you can catch glimpses of The Knob between the trees. Cross the causeway, climb the steps at 0.7 mile, and gasp at the view from The Knob. Return the way you came to the trail intersection, then stay left (straight) to complete the loop and return to your car.

4
LOWELL HOLLY
RESERVATION TRAIL

Type of hike: Out-and-back with loop.
Total distance: 3.8 miles.
Maps: USGS Sandwich.
Jurisdiction: The Trustees of Reservations.
Starting point: South Sandwich Road, Mashpee.
Finding the trailhead: To reach the Lowell Holly Reservation from U.S. Highway 6, Exit 2, go south on Massachusetts 130 for 1.5 miles. Turn left on Cotuit Road for 3.5 miles. Turn right on South Sandwich Road for 0.6 mile to the parking lot on the right.

Key points:
0.7   Reach the Wakeby shore
0.9   Begin the Overlook (Wheeler) Trail
1.2   Reach the Mashpee Pond overlook
1.8   Take the Conaumet Point Trail
2.7   Complete the loop

The hike: This 135-acre peninsula divides Wakeby Pond and Mashpee Pond, two of the largest freshwater ponds on Cape Cod. A trail loop circles the two knolls of the peninsula, offering views of the lakes and a diversity of plant life.

Lowell Holly Reservation Trail

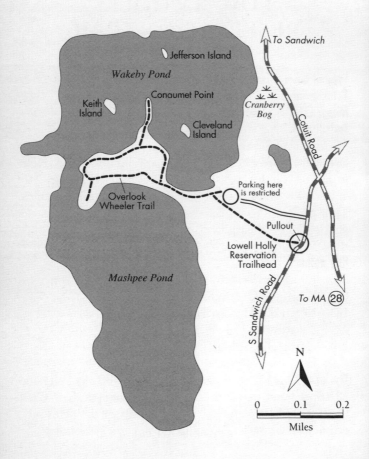

Sweet gum, unique mosses, and ferns thrive here, along with the common day lily, which grows in the low spots. Woodlands boast massive native American holly trees, stands of American beech, and red maples. Abbott Lawrence Lowell, longtime president of Harvard University, created this preserve as a private garden, enriching it with an array of other hardwoods and plants.

Start on the trail to the right (south) of the information kiosk. Look below and to the left for glimpses of a freshwater marsh. Cross the manmade gully and continue through the forest. Ancient hollies intermingle with oaks, black birch, white and pitch pine.

Reach the Wakeby shore at 0.7 and turn left (west). Pass two small beaches and climb through a grove of beech to a clearing. Turn left (southwest) and follow the carriage path onto the peninsula. At 0.9 mile, stay left (west) at the Y intersection. Follow orange blazes marking the Overlook (Wheeler) Trail.

Turn left (south) at the second trail intersection at 1.2 miles for a short walk over slightly elevated land, peeking through openings in the trees for views of Mashpee Pond. Rejoin Overlook Trail and turn left (west). Watch for "turkey tails," a pore fungi, growing on downed trees.

Bear left (north) at the trail crossing at 1.8 miles, exploring Conaumet Point, a narrow spit of land dividing Mashpee and Wakeby ponds. Once back on Overlook Trail, turn left (east), following white blazes down to the shoreline. Complete the loop at 2.7 miles.

Return by retracing your steps past the small parking area and up into the forest, returning to the trailhead.

5
LONG RIVER TRAIL IN THE
MASHPEE RIVER WOODLANDS

Type of hike: Out-and-back.
Total distance: 5.2 miles.
Maps: USGS Cotuit.
Jurisdiction: Mashpee Conservation Commission.
Starting point: Mashpee River Woodlands North Trailhead, Mashpee.
Finding the trailhead: To reach the Mashpee River Woodlands from U.S. Highway 6, Exit 2, go south on Massachusetts 130 for 7.5 miles. Turn right (south) onto Great Neck Road for 2.2 miles to the Mashpee Rotary. Go around the rotary to Massachusetts 28, heading east to Hyannis. Go 0.4 mile to a right turn onto Quinaquissett Avenue, and take an immediate right into Mashpee River Woodlands North parking area.

Key points:
0.6   Take the left (south) fork at the trail intersection
1.8   Reach Marsters Grove
2.0   Follow the Chickadee Trail
2.6   Three trails intersect
2.8   Reach the Whitcomb's Landing Trail
3.2   Rejoin the Long River Trail

The hike: This hike takes you along the contours of hills rising above the four-mile-long Mashpee River. Lined with tall cattails, the river bends several times, providing vistas that are unparalleled.

Conservation lands totalling 689 acres protect the undeveloped wooded shoreline and pristine river for nesting and migrating songbirds, hungry herons, and other native species. Listen for the calls of rufous-sided towhees (drink-your-tea) and look for flickers, the only woodpeckers that feed on the ground.

The Mashpee River is one of the finest sea-run brook trout streams in Massachusetts. The best fishing is from the other bank of the river, which is also protected.

Depart from the left side of the information kiosk on the west side of the parking area. Follow the Long River Trail left (south), through a small clearing. Pass a grove of azaleas and rhododendrons on your left as you descend toward the river, climbing up and scampering down the well-worn sandy trail through a hardwood forest.

At 0.6 mile, take the left (south) fork when the trail splits. Continue up and down, catching glimpses of the Mashpee River through the trees. Pass a towering pitch pine. The trail hooks left (east), dropping into a gully and returning to the river bluff. Take short detours on lookout trails for views of the river and marsh.

A wooden sign for Marsters Grove is posted at 1.8 miles in a stand of pine on the right, giving tribute to the individual who sold 290 acres along the river to the Town of Mashpee. At 2.0 miles, you'll reach a trail marker. Stay riverside (south) following the Chickadee Trail. Private boat docks across the river indicate the boundary of the woodlands.

Another trail marker points to the Partridge Berry Trail. Stay on the Chickadee (now headed east) and continue into the depths of the woods. At 2.6 miles, three trails converge at an information kiosk near the Mashpee River Woodlands south parking area. Go left (north): the trail is not marked. At 2.8 miles, the trail intersects Whitcomb's Landing Trail. Turn left (west) and head back toward the river. Rejoin the Long River Trail at 3.2 miles and retrace your steps to the parking area.

Long River Trail in the Mashpee River Woodlands, Crocker Neck Conservation Area Trail

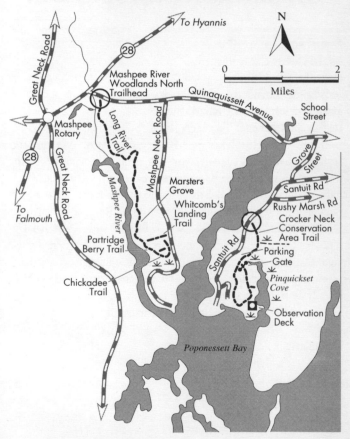

6
CROCKER NECK
CONSERVATION AREA TRAIL

See map on page 23

Type of hike: Loop.
Total distance: 2.2 miles.
Maps: USGS Cotuit.
Jurisdiction: Barnstable Conservation Commission.
Starting point: Santuit Road, Barnstable.
Finding the trailhead: To reach the Crocker Neck Conservation Area from the Mashpee Rotary, go east on Massachusetts 28 toward Hyannis for 0.4 mile. Turn right onto Quinaquissett Avenue. Continue southeast for 1.9 miles (the road turns into School Street just past the bay). Turn right (south) on Grove Street for 0.3 mile to its end at Santuit Road. Follow Santuit Road south for 0.7 mile, past Rushy Marsh Road, to the entrance on the left. The parking is very limited; you may have to continue south on Santuit around the bend for 0.3 mile to a narrow dirt road on the left. It is marked with a conservation sign and a parking area is 0.1 mile further down the dirt road.

Key points:
0.3   Pass a clearing
0.6   Narrow trail ends
0.8   The main trail ends in a circle
0.9   Reach the beach
1.3   Return to the parking area

The hike: Bordered by water on two sides, this lovely 97-acre site was rescued from development in 1985. Named for the Crocker family, early settlers in the town of Barnstable, Crocker Neck includes woodland, salt marsh, freshwater marsh, shrub swamp, estuarine flats, and a small beach.

Markers call attention to some of the unique features of the area. The lower one-mile loop is easy walking, although some of the trail is soft sand. The upper trail is slightly hilly, with native holly dotting the landscape of pine and oak woods. Underbrush of blueberry and huckleberry form a knee-high green hedge.

An observation deck is the perfect vantage point from which to watch herons or catch a glimpse of a great horned owl. Look for tiny minnows in the water or catch fiddler crabs before they dart into their burrows. Bring a picnic to enjoy at one of the stops along the way.

The trail begins at the large sign on Santuit Road. (If you parked in the lot down the dirt road, you'll start by passing through a gray gate to marker 6.) Pass the gate and walk southeast on the sandy path for 0.3 mile, reaching an open area—probably a century-old sand barrow pit. Walk through the clearing to the southeast corner and follow the narrow trail across the dike into the marsh and marker 4.

Return to the clearing and cross it to the southwest corner, picking up the narrow trail into the woods. Pass marker 5. At the fork turn left (south). The narrow trail ends at 0.6 mile.

Make a sharp left and walk south. (If you've started at the second lot, pass through the gray gate.) Marker 6 draws attention to black huckleberry bushes. A small trail on the right leads into a stand of white pine. Return to the main trail, which ends in a wide circle (0.8 mile). The narrow trail on the right takes you to a small bog. On the left (east) is a picnic area and a beautiful view of Pinquickset Cove. Continue on the trail at the south end of the circle to the observation deck. Watch carefully for the osprey family, then follow the trail 0.1 mile south to a small sandy clearing.

Descend to the small wading beach (0.9 mile). After you've rested on the beach, take the left trail straight north to the parking area (1.3 miles). You'll arc sharply right toward the gray gate; at marker 6, make a sharp left and retrace your steps back into the clearing and up to your car.

7
THE OLD BRIAR PATCH TRAIL

Type of hike: Loop.
Total distance: 2.1 miles.
Maps: USGS Sandwich.
Jurisdiction: Green Briar Nature Center.
Starting point: Green Briar Nature Center, Sandwich.
Finding the trailhead: To reach The Green Briar Nature Center from U.S.. Highway 6, Exit 3, travel north on Quaker Meeting House Road for 1 mile to Massachusetts 6A. Turn left (west) for 0.6 mile to Discovery Hill Road. Turn left (south) 0.2 mile to the center's parking area.

Key points:
0.4   Climb the Steep Hill Trail
0.9   Walk the Gully Lane Trail
1.1   Head down the Discovery Loop Trail
1.4   Return on the Briar Patch Trail

The hike: Born in Sandwich on January 4, 1874, author Thornton W. Burgess, creator of the fictional characters of The Old Briar Patch, spent his youth exploring the wilds of Gully Lane. Writing whimsical animal stories for his small son led Burgess to become the noted author of 170 children's books and 15,000 bedtime stories. The Briar Patch Conservation area was dedicated by the Town of Sandwich in 1974 to permanently preserve the rolling hills and swampy lowland home of the many animals that inspired Burgess.

Named for the bull briars that form dense thickets wherever old pastures revert to woodlands, the Old Briar Patch is intertwined with marked trails that wander through a diversity of plant life. The Green Briar Nature Center, with its award-winning wildflower garden, herb garden, and frontage on the "Smiling Pool" pond, provides an delightful and interesting beginning.

The best way to enjoy this trail is to bring a Burgess story with you. Stop and read, then watch and listen for Peter and Mrs. Rabbit, Sammy Jay, Reddy Fox, Old Mr. Toad, Jimmy Skunk, or Bobby Coon.

The trail begins in the southwest corner of the parking area and is marked Briar Patch Trail. Follow it across the water district road and along the ledge behind the water district building for 0.4 mile to the first major intersection marked Steep Hill Trail. Turn right (south) and head up Steep Hill. At the top of the hill turn left (southeast), back into the woods. (For a shorter loop around the pond, stay to the left at each trail intersection.)

Take the right (west) fork when the trail splits. Pass across the water pipe into the woods. The trail meets the Gully Lane Trail at 0.9 mile. Turn left (southeast) on Gully Lane Trail, which veers to the right, reaching a three-way fork in the midst of a grove of black locust trees. Arc sharply right (south) at 1.1 miles onto Discovery Hill Loop. Climb Discovery Hill into a grove of white pines.

Catch glimpses of the swamp below as you descend Discovery Hill. At the base of the hill at 1.4 miles, turn left (west) onto the Briar Patch Trail. This trail follows the wetland on the right. You will pass by the remains of an old boardwalk and through tupelos and beech. Shortly after you pass the Discover Hill Loop trail and a bench on the left, the Briar Patch Trail takes a sharp right. The trail turns left up the steep hill just behind a water district building. Continue past the intersection with Steep Hill Trail, retracing your steps back to Green Briar Nature Center.

The Old Briar Patch Trail

8
THE TRAILS AT SANDY NECK BARRIER BEACH

Type of hike: Loop.
Total distance: 5.25 miles.
Maps: USGS Hyannis.
Jurisdiction: Town of Barnstable.
Starting point: Sandy Neck Beach parking area, West Barnstable.
Finding the trailhead: To reach the Sandy Neck Nature Trail from U.S. Highway 6, Exit 3, travel north on Quaker Meeting House Road for 1 mile to Massachusetts 6A. Turn right (east) and go 3.1 miles to Sandy Neck Road. Turn left for 0.9 mile to the Ranger Station Guard House. Pay the fee and continue for another quarter-mile to the paved parking area.

Key points:
0.3   Reach the Sandy Neck nature trail
0.9   Pass the Trail 1 intersection
1.5   Pass the small private marsh island
2.4   At the Trail 2 intersection, turn toward the beach
2.7   Walk on the beach

The hike: This barrier beach and the surrounding 3,000-acre Great Marsh is the most extensive conservation area out-

The Trails at Sandy Neck Barrier Beach

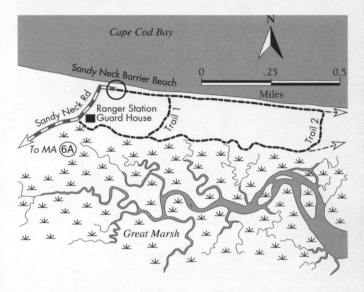

side of the Cape Cod National Seashore, and the largest salt marsh complex on the Cape. The Great Marsh supports an abundance of marine life and provides protection and food for both sea and land birds.

Watch for great blue herons, willets, egrets, and other wading birds. Red-tailed hawks, kestrels, harriers, and other raptors may rise from the tall grasses. On the outer dunes and beach, look for the endangered piping plover or diamondback terrapin.

Unfortunately for human visitors, many insects also thrive in this environment. In an ill-conceived effort to control the bug population, long straight ditches were cut through the marsh to drain standing water. Today, raised wooden boxes trap the greenhead or horse fly. Swallows, which feed on the flies, are attracted to nesting boxes along the trail. The insects still can be annoying here, so remember to wear insect repellent.

Soft sand makes this a more difficult hike. The sun can become unbearably hot and there is little shelter. Start early in the day and carry plenty of water. Prepare to be awed by the dunes, which peak high above you, as well as by the primitive, stubborn plant life and the isolated vastness of the marsh.

Begin by walking back (south), down the road for 0.3 mile from the parking area to the guard house. The area is open to hunting for periods during the fall and winter—check with a Ranger before hiking. Directly across from the off-road vehicle entrance is a small wild cranberry bog. The trail begins opposite the guard house on the east side. Walk in the soft sand east along the Great Marsh.

At 0.9 mile, a mound of wild roses forms an island at the intersection with Trail 1. Stay right (east), following the contours of the marsh. The small island on your right (south) is private. Take the left (east) fork at 1.5 miles and do not trespass.

You have been skirting the secondary or back dunes. Large bare areas called "blowouts" often are caused by human abuse. Wild cherry, red cedar, greenbrier, Virginia creeper, and honeysuckle blend with the more common pitch pine, bearberry, beach plum, and bayberry in the thickets. Small "fish houses" come into view. Families owned these cottages long before the land was set aside as a reserve. At 2.4 miles, turn left (north) into the dunes at the Y intersection (Trail 2).

Just past the secondary dunes, you enter the interdune swale. Less windy, the temperatures are warmer and the ground more arid. Pass through the primary dunes onto the beach (2.7 miles). Turn left (west), walking near the waterline to cool down. Stop for a rest or to picnic and take your time returning to climb the steps to the comfort station and parking area.

Option: Hike further out on "the neck" into more remote areas. Inquire at the ranger station for more information.

The Middle Cape

If Cape Cod had a hub, the Middle Cape would be it. With its train station, ferry terminal, and airport, many travelers begin their visits here. Long and narrow, the Mid Cape includes the towns of Barnstable, Yarmouth, Dennis, Brewster, Harwich, Chatham and Orleans.

The Mid Cape is generally flat and riddled with kettle ponds. Formed when dense glacial ice chunks melted among debris, these ponds vary in size and each one has its own personality. The relentless waves and wind that the terrain must absorb accounts for the Mid Cape's unique stunted vegetation of pitch pine, beech, and scrub oak. Tidal marshlands reach golden fingers to the sea and teem with migrating birds.

The north side retains its original early-American look, with tidy cottages tucked in the woods facing the sea, while the south side is known for warmer water and sunny beaches. Venturing beyond the famous shops and restaurants of the Mid Cape, its quieter spots will inspire you to return again and again.

9
CALLEY-DARLING
CONSERVATION TRAILS

Type of hike: Loop.
Total distance: 2 miles.
Maps: USGS Dennis.
Jurisdiction: Yarmouth Department of Natural Resources.
Starting point: Alms House Road, Yarmouth.
Finding the trailhead: To reach the Calley-Darling Conservation Trails from U.S. Highway 6, Exit 8, go north on Union Street for 1.2 miles to Massachusetts 6A. Zigzag across MA 6A north onto Old Church Road, which you will follow for 0.3 mile, until the road ends at Center Street. Turn right and follow Center for 0.7 mile to Alms House Road. Turn left; the small parking lot is an immediate right.

Key points:
0.4   Walk out on the boardwalk
1.3   Reach the marsh

The hike: Several trails wind through woodlands and across salt marshes in this narrow strip of conservation land. Beautiful and serene, the showstopper here is Gray's Beach, with its spectacular dunes and half-mile boardwalk. Although not really much of a beach, this is a playground for all who love shallow warm water.

Crabs, shrimp, and starfish dance in the sand between marsh and beach grass. The tide whispers into this incredible bay, lapping the grasses into motion. Mesmerizing and delightful, it is difficult to leave.

This trail is a flat and easy loop with diversity around every corner. Check the tides before you go. High tide makes many spots soupy. Bring binoculars and a magnifying glass so you can catch all the sights, from magnificent shore birds and herons to tiny marsh creatures.

The trail begins in the northeast corner of the parking area. A map of the trails is posted just beyond the trailhead. Take the left fork, north through lowlands. Turn left onto Center Street and walk 0.4 mile past the parking lot to the water and the boardwalk.

Stroll out onto the boardwalk all the way to the benches at its end (0.6 mile round-trip). Enjoy the sea breeze and the incredible view before you return to the parking lot.

Cut across the parking area to the grassy hill. Circle the picnic pavilion, walk past the small playground (unless you are with little ones), and head to the trailhead in the southeast corner of the clearing (1.3 miles). The trail leads out into the saltwater marsh; boards have been placed to help you keep your feet dry. Jump the small drainage ditch, circle to your left through ten-foot high phragmites reeds, and climb up to higher ground.

Turn right at the first trail fork, then right again at the next trail intersection, heading west. The woodlands of pine and oak sparkle with holly and pine needles cushion the trail. Scamper down the steps to cross Center Street and return to the parking area.

Calley-Darling Conservation Trails

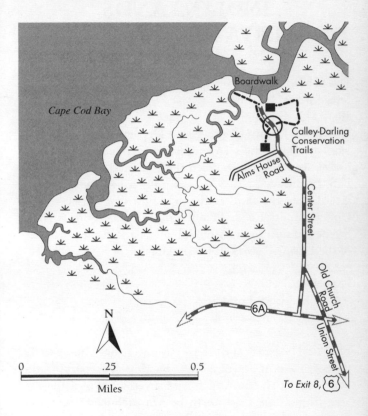

Cape Cod Bay

Boardwalk

Calley-Darling
Conservation
Trails

Alms House Road

Center Street

Old Church Road

Union Street

6A

N

0   .25   0.5
Miles

To Exit 8, 6

10
INDIAN LANDS
CONSERVATION AREA TRAIL

Type of hike: Loop.
Total distance: 1.7 miles.
Maps: USGS Dennis.
Jurisdiction: Dennis Conservation Department.
Starting point: Dennis Town Offices, Dennis.
Finding the trailhead: To reach the Indian Lands Trail from U.S. Highway 6, Exit 9, go south 0.9 miles on Massachusetts 134 to the third traffic light. Turn right (west) onto Upper County Road. Take the right (north) fork to Main Street and turn right. After 0.2 mile, park in the north side of the Dennis Town Offices parking lot.

Key points:
0.4   The wooded trail begins
1.0   Reach the overlook

The hike: The banks of the Bass River were once home to the Pawkannawkut Indians, a tribe that was part of the Wampanoag Nation, which held sovereignty over the vast area from Cape Cod north to Massachusetts Bay. The Pawkannawkut camped and hunted along the river shores until a smallpox epidemic wiped out the tribe in the 1770s. They called their home Mattacheset, meaning "old or plant-

Indian Lands Conservation

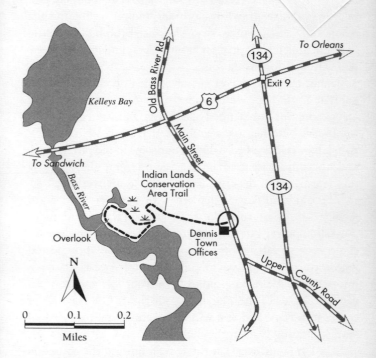

ing lands by the borders of the water." They planted beans, pumpkins, and corn in natural and manmade clearings.

Later, settlers harvested soft salt marsh hay. They cut and piled it on horse-drawn wagons and took it to the uplands where they laid it out to dry. They used the hay for cattle feed and mulch and spread it around the foundations of their drafty homes for insulation.

Today, the Bass River marsh is an important wetland habitat. Cattails provide tender roots for muskrats to eat and perches for red-winged blackbirds. This trail allows you to observe blue herons, search for tree swallows, or watch marsh hawks. Needles cushion your steps in the pitch pines, and it becomes easy to imagine a dugout canoe gliding softly on the expanse of the river as you relax at an overlook.

The trailhead is well-marked with a conservation sign. A wide sandy path runs alongside railroad tracks and under powerline poles. The wooded trail begins at 0.4 mile, over the rise. Turn left (south) onto the trail. A map is posted before you enter the woodlands. Stay left (west) at the Y intersection. A brackish pond is on your left and you can catch glimpses of the marsh to your right. The Bass River comes into view, and you will walk across a narrow strip of land separating it from the marsh.

Stay left (southwest) at the fork, following the shoreline of the Bass River. In the distance you can see cars traveling across a bridge, and as you make a sweeping right turn, beautiful homes with private docks come into view.

A bench perches on a lovely overlook at the 1.0 mile point. Continue north on the path to the marsh. Walk quietly around the sharp right (east) turn—the birds are easily startled. Scan the expanse of marsh for ducks of all varieties and three different types of heron. Before you know it, you will have completed the loop.

Turn left (north), crossing back over the dike and past the brackish pond to the first trail intersection. Stay right (north) to the powerlines. Turn right again to return to the parking area.

11

THE TRAILS AT THE CAPE COD MUSEUM OF NATURAL HISTORY

Type of hike: Two loops.
Total distance: 2.8 miles.
Maps: USGS Harwich.
Jurisdiction: Cape Cod Museum of Natural History.
Starting point: Cape Cod Museum of Natural History, Brewster.
Finding the trailhead: To reach the Cape Cod Museum of Natural History, from U.S. Highway 6, Exit 9, go north on Massachusetts 134 for 3.9 miles to Massachusetts 6A. Turn right (east) for 2.5 miles to the well-marked entrance to the Cape Cod Museum of Natural History parking lot.

The hikes: Three excellent trails, all within the Stony Brook watershed, offer a wonderful introduction to the diversity of the Cape landscape. Walk through upland woods, across salt marshes, near fresh and saltwater creeks, or stretch your toes in a sandy beach. Truly offering something for everyone, from a short, easy loop to challenging hills, these are Cape must-dos. Two of the trails—the John Wing Trail and the South Trail—are described here.

The North Trail is a short, 0.25-mile loop perfect for the very young. Numbered stations identify native flora. Wild-

The Trails at the Cape Cod
Museum of Natural History

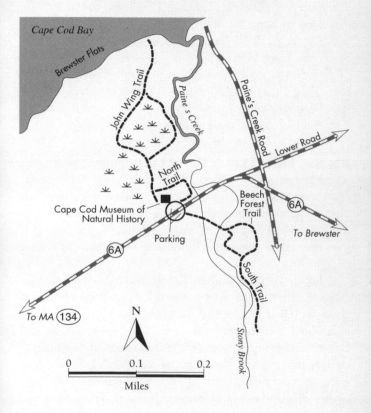

flowers flourish and the views of the salt marsh and Paine's Creek are breathtaking.

The John Wing Trail explores Wing Island, once the site of a farm and saltworks. Inhabited by 1653, the island was first used to harvest salt hay. The trail crosses the marsh, winds through the uplands and then descends to a barrier beach and Cape Cod Bay.

The South Trail passes through a salt marsh and over Paine's Creek, a major migration route for alewives or Cape Cod herring. Pilgrims used alewives as food and to fertilize corn fields. Circle through an unique beech forest to the eastern bank of Stony Brook.

John Wing Trail (1.3 miles): The trail begins on the northwest side of the museum buildings. A boardwalk crosses the marsh (high tide may flood the walkway—check with museum staff). A sign welcomes you to Wing Island. Turn right (east) at marker 4. A monument to John Wing is on the right. Pass through a clearing of tall cedars and then through a hedge.

Make a sharp left at the trail fork and hike north along a ridge. At the top of the rise, turn left (the right fork is a short path to an overlook of Brewster Flats). The trail winds into a pitch pine forest.

Turn right (north) at the trail intersection, then continue straight past marker 7 to an overlook (0.7 mile). For a longer walk, climb down around massive boulders and cross the marsh on one of the well-worn trails to reach the beach. Or, to complete this loop, you can walk back past marker 7 and turn right (southwest) at the first trail crossing, then left (south) at the next intersection. Follow the trail straight ahead, across the marsh to the parking area.

The South Trail (1.5 miles): This trail begins across Massachusetts 6A from the museum on the southeast side of the overflow parking area. Descend to the salt marsh and cross Paine's Creek, then make a sharp left and climb up into the beech forest.

Walk along a ledge above the creek and through a gully to a sharp right turn. The path becomes needle-cushioned as you reach the top of the Beech Forest Loop. Stay left (south) at the Y intersection and descend toward Stony Brook. Take a left at the trail fork; at the next intersection, go right to a lovely overlook.

The trail arcs sharply right into dense thickets. Wind through the lowlands; the thickets give way to lush ferns as you approach the bank of Stony Brook. Pause to admire the brook at 0.9 mile, then turn around and retrace your steps past the overlook to the first Y intersection. Go left and uphill, then drop to the main trail. Walk across the marsh and up to the parking area.

12
THE TRAIL AT HARDING'S BEACH

Type of hike: Loop.
Total distance: 2 miles.
Maps: USGS Chatham.
Jurisdiction: Chatham Planning Board.
Starting point: Harding's Beach parking area, Chatham.
Finding the trailhead: To reach Harding's Beach from U.S. Highway 6, Exit 11, go south on Massachusetts 137 for 3.2 miles. MA 137 ends at Massachusetts 28; turn left (east) and drive for 1.5 miles. Turn right (south) at the blinking light onto Barn Hill Road. Go 0.4 mile and bear right at the fork onto Harding's Beach Road. Follow this 0.9 mile to the beach entrance (a seasonal parking fee is charged). Drive through the first lot into the smaller lot. The trail begins as a soft sand road at the south end of the lot.

Key points:
1.0   Pass the lighthouse driveway

The hike: This is the perfect sunset beach stroll. Harding's Beach is a spit of sand dividing the ocean from Oyster River and Stage Harbor. Plan to watch the sun melt into Nantucket Sound or bring a picnic and stay the day.

A tribute to Chatham's history with the sea, Harding's

The Trail at Harding's Beach, Morris Island Trail

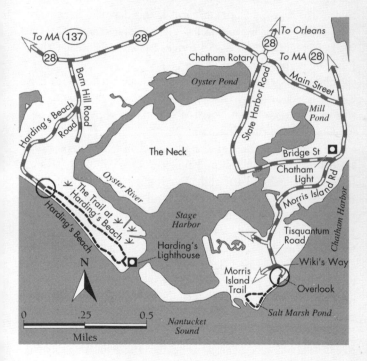

Light has stood sentry at the entrance to Stage Harbor for hundreds of years. Privately owned, it was marred by a storm that toppled the top of the light itself.

In Oyster River, a saltwater inlet, fishermen grow and harvest oysters and naturally flourishing bay scallops. Common terns dive for their next meal, and if you're lucky, you may see a pair of horned larks. This lark is attracted by the sparsely vegetated land and moves by walking rather than hopping across the sand.

The views are spectacular. Across Nantucket Sound is low, sandy Monomoy Island. Directly across the harbor entrance is Morris Island, which is actually a peninsula extending south from Chatham.

To begin, slog through the soft sand on the road past salt spray roses and beach plum. Enjoy the views of Oyster River to your left. Stay to the right when the road forks, staying southeast and out of the marsh. Sand is replaced by gravel, which makes the walking easier. Stage Harbor opens in front and to the left of you, with its small fishing boats secure at their moorings.

Follow the roadbed right (west). The left road at the 1.0 mile point is the private driveway for Harding's Light. Pass in front of the lighthouse, through the dunes and onto the beach. Head north past a small tidal pool.

Roll up your pant legs, sink your toes into the sand, and relish the cool surf. Search for perfect shells in the seaweed mounds left by the last high tide, or watch fiddler crabs dance close to the water. Take some time to savor the beauty of this stretch of white sand before returning to your car.

13
MORRIS ISLAND TRAIL

See map on page 47

Type of hike: Loop.
Total distance: 1.4 miles.
Maps: USGS Chatham.
Jurisdiction: Monomoy National Wildlife Refuge.
Starting point: Monomoy National Wildlife Refuge Headquarters, Chatham.
Finding the trailhead: To reach the Morris Island Trail from Massachusetts Highway 28 at the Chatham Rotary, go straight (east) onto Main Street and follow it 0.9 mile to its end. Turn right on the unmarked extension of Main Street. Go 0.5 mile, past Chatham Light and the parking area. Curve to the right, then take the first left onto Morris Island Road. Drive 1.0 mile to Tisquantum Road and turn left (follow the Monomoy National Wildlife Refuge signs). Turn left on Wiki's Way into the parking lot.

Key points:
0.4 Take the trail inland
1.0 Complete the loop

The hike: Morris Island offers a small sampling of the unique habitats of the Monomoy Islands and is the only section of Monomoy National Wildlife Refuge accessible by land. Countless shore birds, waterfowl, and songbirds rest, feed and nurture their young here. During certain times of the year, seals frolic offshore in the shallow waters.

Monomoy once was a peninsula, then an island, and is now two islands. The constant shifting of sand and sea is evident in the refuge and provides a wonderful introduction to the Cape's seashore and its inhabitants. Gentle waves wash the white sand beach, making it a perfect playground for little ones.

A note: The trail is closed for one hour before and one hour after high tide. Check tide charts before you leave.

Begin by following the trail to the cliff overlooking North and South Monomoy Islands and get an overview of your excursion. Return to the main trail, which descends steep steps and navigates through a tangle of downed trees to the beach.

After chasing the surf and inspecting the shore for treasures, a sign directs you to the trail, which is cut through the dunes to the right (0.4 mile). Stop to read the informational signs, which start in the stabilized dunes, before heading into an area of woody plants behind the dunes, which are protected from the open waters.

The Salt Marsh Pond, with its tall grasses and reeds, is habitat for numerous shore birds and some ocean fish. Follow the trail as it rims the marsh and complete the loop at 1.0 mile back on the beach. If you choose, linger on the beach to rest in the sun or do some beachcombing before heading back up the steps to the parking area.

14
CLIFF POND TRAIL

Type of hike: Loop.
Total distance: 3.9 miles.
Maps: USGS Harwich.
Jurisdiction: Nickerson State Park.
Starting point: East Fishermen's Landing Boat Ramp, Nickerson State Park, Brewster.
Finding the trailhead: To reach the Cliff Pond Trail at Nickerson State Park from U.S. Highway 6, Exit 12, go west on Main Street, away from Orleans. The entrance to the park is 1.6 miles beyond the exit, and is clearly marked. Turn left (south) and drive through the gate. Go 0.2 mile to the sign marked "Area 5." Turn left and travel 0.5 mile past the Area 5 turn-off and Flax Pond Beach. The road ends in a parking area above East Fishermen's Landing Boat Ramp.

Key points:
- 0.9 Pass the north shore boulders
- 1.9 Reach West Fisherman's Landing
- 3.2 Return via the south beach

The hike: Cliff Pond is one of the largest kettle ponds on the Cape. Sandy, crescent-shaped beaches rimmed with pines and oaks glow golden in the sun. The air is crisp with the smell of pine and clear deep water.

The pond is stocked twice each year, attracting fishermen. They wait patiently in their waders along the shore or quietly in small boats or canoes. A still bay on the southern shore and two small pools at either end encourage waterfowl to congregate.

This hike follows the contours of the pond and is made slightly more challenging with climbs in and out of the woods. Long pants will protect your legs from the short brush that threatens to clog some parts of the trail. Many small beaches offer great spots to picnic or relax.

The Cliff Pond trailhead is well-marked on the northwest side of the parking area. Blue blazes mark the trail as it climbs through low brush. A clearing at the top of the hill shelters picnic tables. The trail makes a short right jog and descends a steep bank to the water's edge. The path turns sandy and passes small beaches before heading up into the woods.

The path descends to the shore again, where two giant boulders stand sentry on the north side of the pond (0.9 mile). Cross a ravine created by rain water. A sandy dike separates the pond from a small pool on your right.

At 1.9 miles, you will reach the West Fisherman's Landing parking area. Walk straight across the lot to the southwest corner and follow the trail up into the woods. Turn left (east) at the T intersection onto a wider trail, and left again at the Y intersection following the blue blazes. Cross yet another trail intersection and ascend a small bluff above the pond. Turn left at the next two intersections, using the blue blazes as your guides.

Cliff Pond Trail

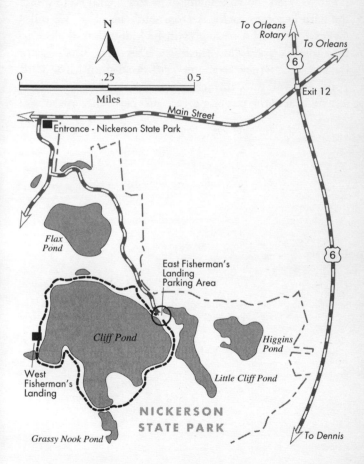

A sandy dike separates Cliff Pond from Grassy Nook Pond. Bear left (north), staying close to the Cliff Pond shore; the path becomes rocky. A large sandy beach at 3.2 miles makes a wonderful resting spot. Pick up the trail close to the shoreline and follow the blue blazes over a small rise to the last dike, which separates Cliff Pond from Little Cliff Pond. You will walk through a wooded area before crossing a small beach; the parking area is just beyond.

The Lower Cape

The Lower Cape or "Outer Cape" is the sandy finger beckoning sailors and travelers to Massachusetts. The tip of Cape Cod, surf-washed and so narrow that at certain points both coasts are visible, has attracted artists for centuries with its unique landscape.

The Cape Cod National Seashore, 27,000 acres of bluffs and sand, occupies more than half of the Lower Cape's land mass and defines the character of this part of Cape Cod. Preserved by John F. Kennedy in 1961, the landscape in this national park constantly changes. Reforestation has begun in many areas, sand dunes are reshaped in every storm, and the tide provides a twice-daily washing of the extensive wetlands.

Whether you are exploring nature's reclaiming of land once tamed by man, becoming awestruck at the vastness of the dunes, or savoring the lingering sun on a deserted beach, the magic of the sand and sea will sweep you up in its beauty.

15
FORT HILL TRAIL

Type of hike: Loop.
Total distance: 1.25 miles.
Maps: USGS Orleans.
Jurisdiction: Cape Cod National Seashore.
Starting point: Penniman House parking area, Cape Cod National Seashore, Eastham.
Finding the trailhead: To reach the Fort Hill Trail, drive 1.5 miles north on U.S. Highway 6 from the Orleans Rotary. At the signs for Fort Hill area turn right (east) onto Governor Prence Road. At the Y intersection, turn left (north) onto Fort Hill Road. Pass the Penniman House on the right and park in the small lot just past it on the left (0.3 mile total from U.S. Highway 6).

Key points:
0.3   Go left (north) where the trail splits
0.7   Reach a trail intersection
0.8   Climb Skiff Hill

The hike: In addition to tremendous vistas, this trail offers a good workout and spectacular birding. Great blue herons sweep over the marsh and songbirds fill the air with their sweet voices. Wander through the Red Maple Swamp, where boardwalks curl through cinnamon and wood ferns under aged red maples.

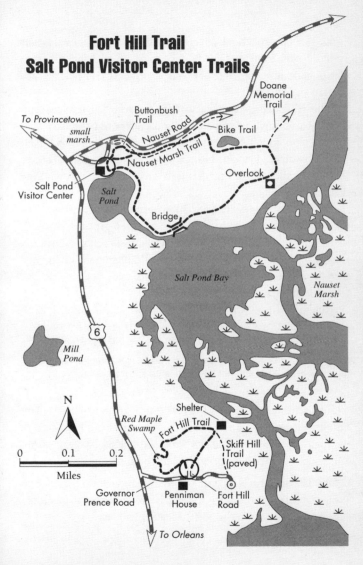

Fort Hill Trail
Salt Pond Visitor Center Trails

To Provincetown

small marsh

Buttonbush Trail

Nauset Road

Bike Trail

Doane Memorial Trail

Nauset Marsh Trail

Salt Pond Visitor Center

Salt Pond

Overlook

Bridge

Salt Pond Bay

Nauset Marsh

US 6

Mill Pond

N

0   0.1   0.2

Miles

Red Maple Swamp

Fort Hill Trail

Shelter

Skiff Hill Trail (paved)

Governor Prence Road

Penniman House

Fort Hill Road

To Orleans

Edge Nauset Marsh, ascend Skiff Hill and puzzle over Indian Rock. Found at the base of the cliff, without the benefit of surrounding artifacts, its unique scratched surface remains a mystery.

The trail begins at the northeast corner of the parking lot. Climb a few log steps up to a meadow. At the first trail intersection, turn left (west), following the sign marked "Red Maple Swamp." Descend into the swamp down a set of steps. A boardwalk meanders through and around the shallow water.

At 0.3 mile, go left (north) where the trail splits. Another section of boardwalk leads to drier ground through hedges of fox grapes. The trail twists and turns, eventually making a sharp right, heading east. Planks again keep your feet dry. Notice new ones are made of recycled plastic before the boardwalk ends.

Reach a three-way trail intersection at 0.7 mile. Climb straight (east) up the short hill to the paved pathway. Turn right (south) and stroll out to the overlook for a rest and a breathtaking view. When you're ready, continue on the paved path up (east) to Skiff Hill at 0.8 mile. Enjoy the view and scan Nauset Marsh for birds.

From the shelter, head down (straight southwest). You quickly come out of the woods, walking along the edge of the meadow. Pass the first trail crossing to Red Maple Swamp and retrace your steps downhill to the parking area.

Option: During the season, take the time to visit the Penniman House. Highlighted with a whalebone archway, this Victorian home was once the most elegant in Eastham.

16
SALT POND VISITOR
CENTER TRAILS

Type of hike: Loop.

See map on page 57

Total distance: 1.25 miles.
Maps: USGS Orleans.
Jurisdiction: Cape Cod National Seashore.
Starting point: Salt Pond Visitor Center, Cape Cod National
Seashore, Eastham.
Finding the trailhead: To reach the Salt Pond Visitor Center,
follow U.S. Highway 6 north from the Orleans Rotary for
3.1 miles. Turn right at the well-marked visitor center en-
trance on Nauset Road. The parking area is 0.1 mile on the
right.

The hikes: The Buttonbush Trail, 0.25 mile long, is designed
for the visually impaired. This is a trail of contrasting sur-
faces, sudden temperature changes and plenty of sounds.
Equipped with Braille and large-print markers, this flat easy
trail circles Buttonbush Pond, offering an interesting introduction to its inhabitants.

The Nauset Marsh Trail includes half of the Buttonbush
Trail, so it isn't necessary to do both. Gradual ascents weave
through gentle rolling countryside filled with cedars and
bayberries; the path dips down to wind along the shoreline
of Nauset Marsh and Salt Pond. Overlooks offer you the
chance to reflect on expansive, water-filled views.

Each decade brings change to the Nauset Marsh. The buildup of the narrow barrier beach, Nauset Spit, allows the marsh to flourish, and the ocean formed a narrow channel linking an original freshwater pond to the sea, creating Salt Pond. Today, the marsh and pond are home to abundant plant and animal life.

Buttonbush Trail: The trail begins on the upper left (east) side of the amphitheater at the south side of the parking lot. A guide rope leads from marker to marker as you wind around the pond. A boardwalk raises you above the pond's surface. The trail intersects with Nauset Marsh Trail and the bicycle trail.

Cross a small section of trail that does not have a guide rope to complete the loop. A slight rise takes you into a wooded area above the pond. Study the different trees and bushes, both native and introduced. End this delightful trail where you began.

Nauset Marsh Trail: Check with the folks in the visitor center before beginning this hike. During high tide, especially in the spring, the trail may be closed. Start on the lower right side (southwest corner) of the amphitheater at the south side of the parking lot. You quickly reach Salt Pond's shoreline where you turn left (south). Walk the pond's edge, which, depending on the tide, may be dry or spongy masses of salt hay. A boardwalk protects you from all but the highest tide on the far end of the pond.

Curve sharply to the left (southeast) along the flow of sea water entering the pond. Make a gradual ascent, following the ledge around another left (eastward) curve. Cross the dike on a wooden bridge at 0.4 mile.

Stay right (south) at the trail fork and climb a series of log steps. Stay on the trail, respecting private property. Continue on the log-lined main trail up to a lookout (0.6 mile). If you have the energy, turn right onto the Doane Memorial Trail. It is 0.9 mile each way.

Otherwise, continue straight (east) through the wooded hills. Cross the bike path into an area that had been farmed. Black locust trees were planted here to replenish the soil. Cross the bike path again and then take the right (north) fork of the Buttonbush Trail back to the parking area.

17
GREAT ISLAND TRAIL

Type of hike: Out-and-back.
Total distance: 3.6 miles.
Maps: USGS Wellfleet.
Jurisdiction: Cape Cod National Seashore.
Starting point: Great Island parking area, Kendrick Avenue, Wellfleet.
Finding the trailhead: To reach the Great Island Trail, drive 11.6 miles north on U.S. Highway 6 from the Orleans Rotary to the light at the sign for Wellfleet Center. Turn left onto Main Street for 0.3 mile. Turn left, down the hill, onto Commercial Street for 0.7 mile. At the Town Pier, make a sharp right onto the unmarked road (Kendrick Avenue). Travel on Kendrick Ave. 2.6 miles, staying left at the Y intersection, passing the public beach and going over the causeway. Just beyond the public recreation area lot, turn left at the sign for Great Island.

Key points:
1.8   Reach the tavern site

The hike: This is the one of the most fascinating hikes on Cape Cod. The trail follows a saltwater marsh across a dike of sand that transformed Great Island into a peninsula. Great Island is wild and windswept, with a small stunted pine forest, vast bearberry and lichen-covered dunes, and miles of

Great Island Trail

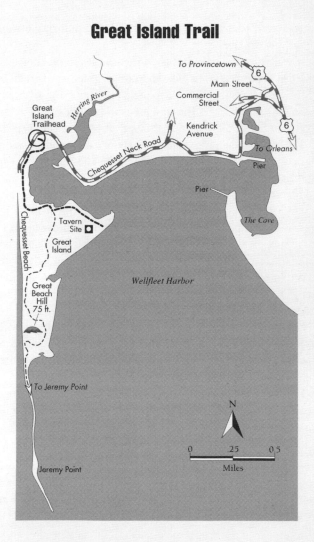

sandy beach that narrow to Jeremy Point, pointing a bony finger toward Brewster.

It was into this bay that the Pilgrims sailed on their second exploration. Later, whalers congregated on Great Island—in fact, some say the name Wellfleet came from the term "Whale Fleet." This trail leads to the site of a whaler's tavern and is one of many options that explore the island.

There is little shade, so start early to avoid midday summer sun. Erosion is a major problem on the island: Stay on established trails and off the fragile dunes.

The trail begins on the left (east) side of the parking area as you enter. Descend on the gravel path to the edge of the marsh. Turn right (west) and circle the marsh on the mud flats. Stay on the inside of the fence, off the dunes. As you make the left (south) turn, you will be on the "gut," the tombolo that connects the peninsula to the mainland. Continue straight past the end of the fence, and turn left (east) again, following the edge of the marsh.

Before you reach the bay, a trail leads into the woods. Follow the trail to the markers at the yet-to-be-excavated tavern (1.8 miles), then return to the main trail at the marsh edge. Retrace your steps back to the gut.

From the northwest corner of the marsh, turn right to return the way you came, around the marsh and up to the parking area.

Options: Plow west through the dunes to Chequesset Beach for some sun, or walk as far south on the beach as you wish. To reach Jeremy Point, you must hike 4.1 miles one-way from the parking area. Much of the point is submerged except at the lowest tide. Consult local tide charts.

18
PILGRIM SPRING TRAIL AND SMALL'S SWAMP TRAIL

Type of hike: Two short loops.
Total distance: 1 mile.
Maps: USGS North Truro.
Jurisdiction: Cape Cod National Seashore.
Starting point: Pilgrim Heights parking area, Cape Cod National Seashore, North Truro.
Finding the trailhead: To reach the Pilgrim Spring and Small's Swamp Trails, follow U.S. Highway 6 for 21.5 miles north from the Orleans Rotary. Turn right onto the road marked Pilgrim Heights. Follow the arrows for 0.5 mile to the parking area near the interpretive shelter. The trails begin at the far end of the parking area near the shelter. If you park in the lower lot, follow the short trail to the upper parking area, do the Small's Swamp Trail and then Pilgrim Spring Trail, which ends in the lower lot.

Key points:
0.2   Reach Pilgrim Spring
0.3   Complete the Pilgrim Spring Trail
0.8   Traverse along the edge of the bluff on the Small's Swamp Trail

The hike: These two trails wind around and above a kettle

Pilgrim Spring Trail and Small's Swamp Trail

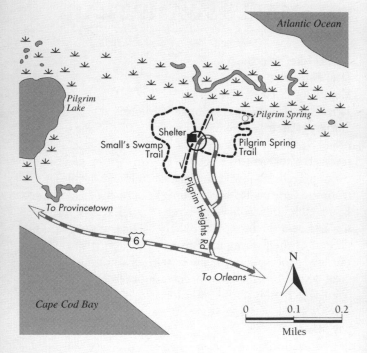

swamp and marsh, which was formed when a buildup of sand closed off the ocean in 1869. An interpretive shelter provides information, and the trails are well-marked with historical and nature signposts. Both trails offer impressive views of East Harbor Creek, Pilgrim Lake, sand dunes, the salt meadow, and the Atlantic Ocean.

Pilgrim Spring Trail leads through a pitch pine forest to Pilgrim Spring. Although historians argue about its exact location and date, a stone marker identifies the probable site of the first fresh water the Pilgrims found. Overlooking a marsh and what's left of East Harbor Creek, the small spring bubbles up near a bramble patch.

Small's Swamp Trail explores the remains of Thomas Small's Farm and circles the kettle swamp. Nothing remains of Small's efforts except his grape, lilac, plum, and apple plantings. Untamed now, they blend with the swamp azaleas, highbush blueberries, bearberries and the returning woods.

Pilgrim Spring Trail: Begin by heading northeast, down into the pitch pine forest of odd, windswept trees. Pine needles make interesting patterns on the sandy trail. Climb up a short rise to an overlook for a breathtaking view. Then, scamper down the trail to the spring and marker at 0.2 mile.

Start the ascent to the parking area southwest of the spring. (The paved trail below is the Head of the Meadow Bicycle Trail.) Climb switchbacks up to the lower parking area. Cross the parking lot, go up the sandy path to the upper lot and back to the shelter (0.3 mile), where you will begin the Small's Swamp Trail.

Small's Swamp Trail: This trail starts by descending to a pitch pine grove. Turn left (west) at the trail fork and follow the rough-hewn fence down the steps and back and forth on the switchbacks into the kettle swamp.

The sandy path goes through a berry patch and circles the swampy lowlands. One long boardwalk keeps you dry across the wettest spot. Enjoy the cool beech forest and then climb the steps cut out of bearberry. Three markers identify features of the outstanding view below as you traverse the edge of the bluff at 0.8 mile.

Head back into the forest. Turn left at the fork and retrace your steps to the parking lot.

19
BEECH FOREST TRAIL

Type of hike: Loop.
Total distance: 1 mile.
Maps: USGS Provincetown.
Jurisdiction: Cape Cod National Seashore.
Starting point: Beech Forest Trail parking area, Cape Cod National Seashore, Provincetown.
Finding the trailhead: To reach the Beech Forest Trail, follow U.S. Highway 6 north for 26.4 miles from the Orleans Rotary. Turn right at the traffic light onto Race Point Road. The Beech Forest Trail parking area is 0.5 mile beyond on the left.

Key points:
0.3   Pass the first trail intersection
0.7   Steps lead down to the pond

The hike: The Beech Forest Trail follows the edges of a freshwater pond, then rambles through a beech forest mixed with native pitch pine and scrub oak.

Thriving forests once blanketed the northernmost tip of Cape Cod, but early settlers showed little concern for natural resources. Clear cutting, overgrazing, and forest fires obliterated the native landscape. By the 1800s, shifting dunes threatened to destroy the Province Lands settlements. Strict conservation controls began and beach grass was planted, stabilizing the dunes' movements.

Now, parts of this vast land have been reforested and fresh water has collected in low spots. Visit the small pond on the return portion of the loop by using short spur trails. Approach quietly to be greeted with the bulging eyes and croaking voices of frogs. Many species of ducks and wading birds call the ponds home and you might catch a glimpse of a turtle.

The salt spray rose, or *rosa rugosa*, thrives in the sandy soil: look for the delicate magenta or white blossoms. In the spring, thick yellow lilies cover the pond's surface.

Be sure to continue past the trailhead on Race Point Road to the visitor's center. The views are well worth the trip.

The trail begins at the northeast corner of the parking lot. Log-lined, it enters the pitch pine forest and traverses on boardwalks over low spots. Soft sand slows your progress through a small clearing.

At the trail intersection at 0.3 mile, go straight into the beech forest. The pathway is paved for a short distance as it winds its way up into the woods.

Steps bring you down to the pond at 0.7 mile. Skirt the opposite bank of the pond and then walk between it and a smaller pond. A small plank wharf provides a resting spot overlooking the smaller pond. The trail ends at the opposite side of the parking area.

Beech Forest Trail

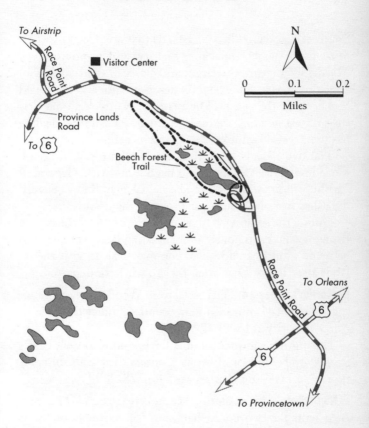

The Islands

South of Cape Cod lie two islands that are different in almost every way: landscape, history, and temperament. Martha's Vineyard, the larger and closer of the two, has an agricultural base. Forest dominates its interior and unspoiled beaches ring the coasts. The island of Nantucket once was the greatest whaling center in the world; economic decline has preserved Nantucket Town and its cobblestone streets.

The two islands share the same glacial roots, although the Nauset Tribe explains their beginnings with a legend of Moshup, their God and legendary whaleman. They believed the ashes from Moshup's pipe formed the islands.

During the summer, both islands are extremely congested. Bringing your car is not recommended, and reservations must be made months in advance. You may wish to visit the islands after Labor Day when the crowds have departed.

To Martha's Vineyard: Ferries sail from Woods Hole to Vineyard Haven (45 minutes) year-round. Contact the Steamship Authority at (508) 477-8600.

During the summer months ferries sail into Oak Bluffs from Woods Hole or Hyannis. Contact the Steamship Authority or Hy-Line Cruises at (508) 778-2600.

To Nantucket: Ferries sail from Hyannis year-round. The "Fast Boat" cuts the two-and-a-half hour trip to one hour, but is more expensive. Contact the Steamship Authority or Hy-Line Cruises.

20
LONG POINT
WILDLIFE REFUGE TRAIL

Type of hike: Loop.
Total distance: 2 miles.
Maps: USGS Tisbury Great Pond.
Jurisdiction: The Trustees of Reservations.
Starting point: Long Point Wildlife Refuge, West Tisbury, Martha's Vineyard.
Finding the trailhead: To reach the Long Point Wildlife Refuge from the ferry during the off-season, drive straight ahead to the stop sign and turn left onto Water Street. At the next stop sign, turn right onto South Main Street. Drive uphill (0.3 mile) to Vineyard Haven/Edgartown Road and turn left (west). Drive 2.3 miles to a blinking light. Turn right onto Airport Road. Follow Airport Road for 2.5 miles until it ends at Edgartown/West Tisbury Road. Turn right (west) on Edgartown/West Tisbury Road for 1.7 miles to Deep Bottom Road. The entrance is well-marked; turn left (south) and follow the signs for 2.6 miles to the parking area.

During season: Follow the directions above to Edgartown/West Tisbury Road. Go west on the Edgartown/West Tisbury Road for 0.3 mile to Waldron's Bottom Road. Turn left (south), and drive for 1.2 miles to the end of the road. Turn left on Scrubby Neck Road and follow it 0.2 mile to Hughe's Thumb Road. Turn right (south) through the gate and drive

Long Point Wildlife Refuge Trail

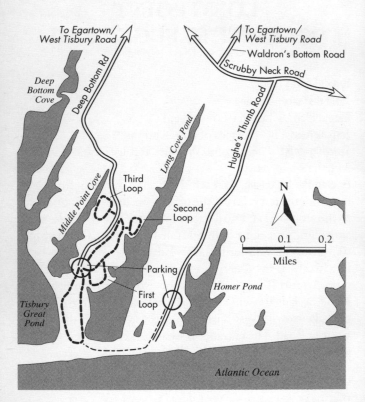

1.25 miles to the parking area (follow the signs). Start by heading north along Long Cove Pond.

Key points:
0.4 Reach the beach
0.7 Pass marker 6
0.8 Complete the first loop
1.1 Reach the second loop
1.7 Complete the third loop

The hike: The 632 acres of this preserve makes it one of the largest on the Vineyard. Primarily dedicated to the protection of wildlife, only part of the preserve is open to the public. A fee is charged during season.

The pine-oak forest opens to one of the best remaining examples of rare coastal sand plains grasslands that stretches to magnificent dunes lining the Atlantic shoreline. From the edge of the woods, long, narrow ponds alternate with fingers of land to create a mix of fresh and brackish waters, salt marsh, and ocean shore. Tisbury Great Pond, with its exquisite white sand beach, is lovely, but requires water shoes for wading because of shell fragments.

Salt spray roses add dashes of pink to the waving grasses and a fragrant scent to the salty air. They attract butterflies and moths of many kinds. Little red-bellied snakes search the ground for earthworms or slugs, and harriers and red-tailed hawks hunt during the day.

An information kiosk marks the start of the trail, which is on the south side of the parking area. Head south and take the right fork. Walk out onto the heath. Cross the roadway. Crushed shells—the remnants of seagulls' dinners—lie on the trail.

Tisbury Great Pond soon comes into view. The saltwater pond is naturally cleansed by the ocean washing over the dike. Walk 0.4 mile to the boardwalk crossing the dunes to the beach. Enjoy the crashing waves before returning up over the barrier beach.

Head north along Long Cove Pond, reaching a trail intersection. Turn right, following the hiking trails sign. Marker 6 at 0.7 mile identifies wild grape vines. Enter a pine and oak forest. Turn right at 0.8 mile and complete the first loop for better views of Long Cove Pond.

Rejoin the main trail and turn right. Continue straight at the trail intersection at 1.1 miles and then make a sharp right to the second short loop through a stand of pitch pines. The overlook is on a spot where archaeologists found evidence of an early native fishing village.

Turn right (northwest), passing a trail intersection and crossing the entrance road. Complete the third loop at 1.7 miles for views of Middle Point Cove. Retrace your steps across the road and turn right (south) at the trail intersection. Walk a short distance back to the parking area.

21
MENEMSHA HILLS
RESERVATION TRAIL

Type of hike: Loop.
Total distance: 3.5 miles.
Maps: USGS Naushon Island and Squibnocket.
Jurisdiction: The Trustees of Reservations.
Starting point: North Road, Chilmark, Martha's Vineyard.
Finding the trailhead: To reach the Menemsha Hills Reservation from the ferry, drive straight ahead to the stop sign and turn left onto Water Street. At the next stop sign, turn right onto South Main Street. Drive uphill past the Vineyard Haven/Edgartown Road. South Main Street becomes State Road in the outskirts of Vineyard Haven. At 2.4 miles, reach the intersection with Old County Road. Go right, continuing on State Road. At 2.6 miles, take the right fork onto North Road and drive west 4.7 miles to the entrance sign and parking area on the right.

Key points:
0.5   Complete the west side of the Harris Trail Loop
0.9   Lower Scenic Trail begins
1.9   Lower Scenic Trail ends
2.1   Pause at the overlook
2.8   Complete Upper Trail loop

Menemsha Hills Reservation Trail

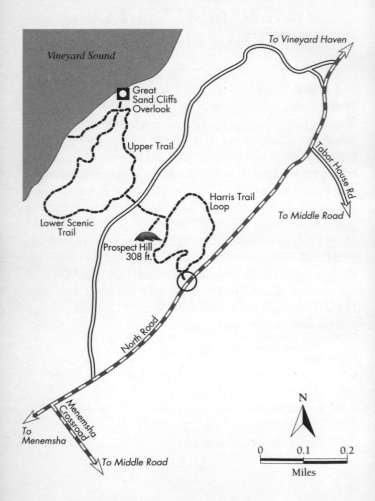

The hike: This hourglass-shaped trail winds through oak woodland and heath that cover the rolling hills sweeping up to the edge of great sand cliffs. Standing 150 feet above a stretch of rocky beach, the cliffs are one of the best places on the island to watch the sunset. Across Vineyard Sound, the Elizabeth Islands, Nobska Point, and the town of Falmouth are visible.

For views of the island, climb to the top of Prospect Hill. The second highest point on the Vineyard, at 308 feet, it offers spectacular views of the village of Menemsha and Aquinnah beyond.

Harbor seals often bask on the beach and waterfowl are a common sight offshore. Deer call the woodlands home and redtail hawks hunt in the heath. For the requested dollar donation per hiker, you can challenge yourself with the greatest change in elevation of any trail on the Vineyard.

The trail begins at an information kiosk on the west side of the parking area. Take the left fork and wind into the deep woods of the Harris Trail Loop.

Complete the west side of the loop at 0.5 mile. Go uphill on the connecting path to the Upper Trail. At the top of the rise, turn left for the short detour to Prospect Hill. Return to the main trail and drop through a stand of oaks and across a dirt roadway.

At the trail intersection at 0.9 mile, turn left onto the Lower Trail, marked Scenic. The terrain is hilly; the trail switches back several times. Descend to an overlook with a magnificent view of the village of Menemsha and Menemsha Pond. Continue through an area of heath, crossing a plank bridge. Descend to a wooden bridge and the end of the Lower Scenic Trail at 1.9 miles.

Make a sharp left at the trail fork, following the yellow blazes. Walk 0.2 mile straight ahead to the Great Sand Cliffs Overlook and gaze out across Vineyard Sound. When you are ready, return to the main trail.

At the trail intersection, go left (uphill) on the Upper Trail. The trail curves right, then south before joining the Lower Scenic Trail at 2.8 miles. Follow the red blazes back across the road, through the wall and up the hill on the connecting trail. Pass the trail to Prospect Hill and descend to the top of the Harris Loop Trail. Make a sharp left. Continue into the lowlands; the trail widens. Join the original trail, turn left and return to your car.

Option: From the Great Sand Cliffs Overlook, follow the trail cut into the steep cliff to the rocky shore below. The trail (0.6 mile round-trip) is difficult, but if you enjoy waves roaring onto rocks, the scenery is great, especially at high tide.

22

THE TRAIL AT TUPANCY LINKS

Type of hike: Loop.
Total distance: 1.25 miles.
Maps: USGS Nantucket.
Jurisdiction: Nantucket Conservation Foundation.
Starting point: Cliff Road, Nantucket.
Finding the trailhead: To reach Tupancy Links from the intersection of Broad Street and North Water Street, drive north on North Water Street in Nantucket Town for 0.2 mile to a three-way intersection. Continue straight ahead and then to the left onto Cliff Road, following Cliff Road west for 1.4 miles to the parking area on the right.

Key points:
0.7   Reach the beach overlook

The hike: The trail at Tupancy Links allows you to walk to the bluff that rises from the sea along the north shore of Nantucket. Cliff Beach, 42 feet below (and inaccessible), is a narrow strip of sand gently washed with the softer waves of the sound.

Bring the binoculars to focus in on Dionis Beach, Eel Point and Tuckernuck Island to the west. Look for Jetties Beach, the entrance to Nantucket Harbor and the skyline

Tupancy Links, Sanford Farm, Ram Pasture and The Woods Trail

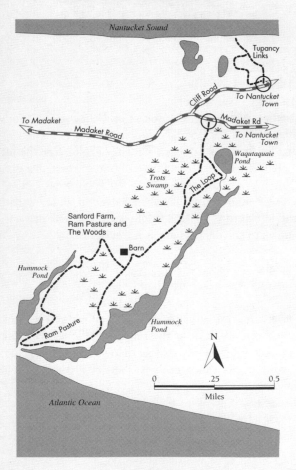

of Nantucket Town against the eastern horizon. Several species of sea birds and ducks frolic in Nantucket Sound.

Stroll through a meadow that was cleared in 1921 to create a golf course. The Nantucket Golf Course expanded to 18 holes, half of which were later donated to the Nantucket Conservation Foundation by Mr. and Mrs. Oswald A. Tupancy.

Nantucket was forested with tall oaks and pines when Europeans landed here in the 17th century. Early settlers cut trees for homes and ships. By 1779, Nantucket had been stripped of forest. For more than a hundred years, sheep grazed on the "Commons," as the moors are known locally. As the sheep declined, sweet pepperbush, highbush blueberry, bayberry, honeysuckle, and broom grew in the sandy soil. It was on this site that Nantucket shadbush was discovered. Originally believed to only exist on Nantucket, this variety of shadbush also grows on Long Island and the barrier beaches of New Jersey. Classified as a "special concern" species, this bush is also known as the juneberry or sugarplum.

Begin by walking through the turnstile; take the right fork uphill. The trail is a cart path, wide enough for partners to walk side-by-side. At the crest of the hill, stop for a sweeping view of rolling hills. Actually dunes stabilized by grass, the short hills are fun to traverse to the first trail intersection. Turn right (north), and ascend to the bluffs (0.7 mile) through a carpet of bearberry, thickets of bayberry, and pasture rose to the overlook area. Do not cross the barrier fence to the cliff edge—it is very dangerous.

Go back south on to the trail intersection, and bear right, heading west on the narrow trail through the beach grass and heath plants. The trail winds near private property and connects to the cart-path loop. Continue straight on the cart path, south across the field to a trail intersection.

Turn left onto the narrow trail and pass through a pitch pine grove to return to the parking area.

23
SANFORD FARM,
RAM PASTURE AND
THE WOODS TRAIL

See map on page 82

Type of hike: Out-and-back with loop.
Total distance: 6.2 miles.
Maps: USGS Nantucket.
Jurisdiction: Nantucket Conservation Foundation
Starting point: Madaket Road, Nantucket
Finding the trailhead: To reach the Sanford Farm and Ram Pasture from Main Street, drive slowly for 0.7 mile on the cobbled street. You'll need the time to savor the sights anyway. At the Soldiers and Sailors Monument, take the right fork onto Upper Main Street for 0.3 mile. The road changes to brick before Caton Circle, which is an intersection of four roads with a flagpole in the center. Bear left (west) onto Madaket Road and drive west for 1.5 miles to the parking area on the left.

Key points:
0.3   Reach the first trail intersection
1.6   Pass the barn
2.9   Go through the stile at beach
4.2   Complete the beach loop
4.9   Reach "The Loop" intersection

The hike: This trail explores the southern half of Nantucket. Walk across a lovely meadow, along the edge of Trots Swamp, a stretch of freshwater wetlands, and into a stand of pitch pines. On top of a rise, a wooden barn stands sentry over an incredible view. Hummock Pond glistens beyond the Ram Pasture, now dotted with osprey nest posts. Rolling dunes separate the two sections of the pond from the Atlantic beach.

Hummock Pond was one U-shaped pond until 1978. During a winter storm, the waves drove enough sand over the dunes to split the pond in two at its narrowest point. Today, the wetland habitat of the ponds attracts waterfowl.

This is a well-marked walk into the agricultural roots of the island. Originally the peninsula, called Nanahuma's Neck for a popular sachem (native chief), was forested. The Sherburne Settlement was established by the English here in 1659. They called the strip surrounded by Hummock Pond Long Woods. Later, settlers felled the trees for pasture. Rams were contained with an elaborate series of high fences and ditches to control the time of year that lambs were born.

The trail begins next to the gate at the southeast side of the parking lot. Follow the dirt road straight south across Sanford Farm's cow pasture to the first trail intersection (0.3 mile), and continue south.

Pass another trail intersection and continue south toward the barn at 1.6 miles, which is a nice place to rest and enjoy the view. After your rest, walk south to the fork at the top of the beach loop.

Turn right along the northern side of the pasture, and come to a trail intersection. Turn left (south) off the roadway onto the narrow trail. Hummock Pond is on your right. Pass the stile in the fence (2.6 miles), then cross the dunes to the beach. Relax nestled in the sand before returning to the pasture.

Follow the fence east toward the other section of Hummock Pond. The trail circles the east side of the pasture and rejoins the main trail at 4.2 miles. From here, retrace your steps up past the barn and down into the wetlands to the base of "The Loop" (4.9 miles). Take the right fork. Pass the Head of Hummock Pond and Waqutaquaie Pond before rejoining the main trail. Turn right to return to the parking area.